INTRODUCTION

THE record books were rewritten once again in season 1993/94 as Rangers became the first side in the Club's long and illustrious history to win six consecutive League Championships and seven domestic trophies in succession. The latter record had never before been achieved by any other club.

Naturally there was disappointment at not having secured historic back-to-back 'Trebles' following the Scottish Cup Final defeat but marvellous memories still remain nevertheless.

Few will forget the amazing events at Parkhead in the traditional Ne'erday encounter against Celtic or that wonderful winning goal in the League Cup Final against Hibernian.

Now, with the arrival at Ibrox of such quality European players as Brian Laudrup of Denmark and Basile Boli of France, further glory beckons.

Written by Douglas G. Russell

Edited by John C. Traynor

Published by

INGLIS ALLEN

The Photographs in this Annual were
supplied by **The Sun**.

Picture Editor:
Mark Sweeney.

Photographers:
Steve Welsh, Alan Ewing, Andy Barr,
Peter Kelly, Mark Sweeney.

Except Pages 4 and 5 which are
reproduced from
BLUE HEAVEN: The Celtic Trophy Room,
published 1989 by Holmes McDougall Ltd.

CONTENTS

A WARRI

SOME call him 'Attila' after the greatest of all the Barbarian kings; a ruler whose warriors became the scourge of the mighty Roman Empire in the 5th century. His nicknames vary from 'The Hit Man' to 'The Dark Destroyer' but one inescapable conclusion remains the same: Mark Hateley will go down as one of the most feared strikers in Scottish football.

His worth to Rangers in Season 1993/94 was incalculable as week after week he put together a series of masterly displays. It came as no great surprise when he was voted 'Scotland's Player of the Year' by the Football Writers' Association – the first Englishman *ever* to win this prestigious award.

As a *creator* of goals, one game in particular springs to mind, against Dundee United at Ibrox in late April 1994. With the Championship still not won and major rivals, Motherwell, 1–0 up at half-time against Hibs, Rangers fell a goal behind early in the second period. It was Hateley who then manufactured both the equalising and winning goals that Gordon Durie converted.

It is *his* goals, of course, that remain longer in the memory . . . the winning strike against Celtic to take 10-man Rangers through to the League Cup Final . . . the two first-half goals that destroyed Aberdeen at Ibrox in the December Premier League encounter . . . his quite delightful left-foot shot that

OR KING

curled past Pat Bonner in the first minute of *that* game at Parkhead . . . the 'double' to finally kill off Kilmarnock in the Scottish Cup semi-final replay. A total of 30 in all competitions.

In years to come, when his playing days are eventually over, there can be no doubt that Mark Hateley will take his rightful place as one of the truly-great Rangers. ⚽

A WARRIOR KING

Hateley soars above Craig Levein of Hearts to win another aerial duel.

A WARRIOR KING

Mark Hateley climbs high above John Inglis to head Rangers' second goal in the 4–0 victory over St Johnstone, Ibrox, March 1994.

SONG SUNG BLUE

IT WAS surely a classic case of the right signing at the right time, as only one week after his debut appearance for Rangers against Partick Thistle at Firhill, Gordon Durie scored both goals (the second, incidentally, a quite delightful header) in a most significant 2–0 away victory against close rivals, Motherwell. His impact could hardly have been more immediate.

Although the player had been linked with Ibrox for some considerable time, Durie's services were finally secured only in late November '93 following a £1.2 million transfer from London club, Tottenham Hotspur. 'Juke Box' eventually tallied 13 goals (including another two doubles against Partick Thistle and Dundee United) in his first season to become Rangers' second-highest scorer after the inimitable Mark Hateley.

Disappointment was written all over his face when he failed to realise the dream of a Scottish Cup winner's medal in the last game of the season but his time will surely come again.

Durie's contribution to the Club since his arrival had been a major one, which is hardly surprising when you consider that he is, indeed, a major league player.

The song says, 'Home is where the heart is'.

WELCOME HOME, GORDON! ⚽

Gordon Durie's first goal in the 2–1 victory over Dundee United, Ibrox, April 1994.
Below: 'Juke Box' heads No.2 past the helpless Van De Kamp.

4

From '94

Top Left: Duncan Ferguson's first goal for Rangers, Ibrox v. Raith Rovers, April '94.

Top Right: Mark Hateley's winning goal in 2–1 victory at Tynecastle, March '94.

Bottom Left: David Robertson's 'wonder strike' which preceded Ferguson's, above.

Bottom Right: Gordon Durie scores in the 5–1 romp v. Partick Thistle, Ibrox, February '94.

A KIND OF

Scottish League Cup Final, 24th October 1993
HIBERNIAN   1   RANGERS   2
Durrant (55 mins)
McCoist (81 mins)

LITTLE did the gathering fans know that the destiny of the season's first trophy would be decided by one of those magical moments that become the stuff of legend.

This was the first time that Rangers and Hibernian had ever met in the League Cup Final, although the Edinburgh club had beaten their Glasgow rivals at the semi-final stage in 1991 on their way to lifting the silverware that year.

Astonishingly, Rangers had graced 10 of the previous 12 League Cup Finals but, rather ominously, on the two occasions they failed to reach it (in 1986 and the aforementioned 1991), it was Hibs who had disposed of them. This season, they had already collected the scalps of Aberdeen and (in a most memorable night at Ibrox when reduced to 10 men) Celtic, on the way to this Final confrontation.

The East of Scotland team took to the field sitting proudly at the top of the Premier Division, two points ahead of Rangers with 12 games played. They had a right to feel confident that this could be their day.

MAGIC

The 'Light Blues' certainly had the better of the first-half exchanges although the interval was reached with both teams having drawn a blank.

The deadlock was finally broken ten minutes into the second period with a quite delightful goal involving Hateley and Durrant in a 'one-two' before 'Blue, White, Dynamite' himself chipped the ball over the advancing Jim Leighton. Many felt that this would certainly seal Hibs' fate but a bizarre own-goal by big Dave McPherson less than five minutes later levelled the score. In fact, minutes later, only a superb goal-line clearance by Gary Stevens kept it that way.

When Pieter Huistra was substituted by Ally McCoist in 67 minutes, it seemed somehow inevitable that the game's decisive and outstanding moment would be courtesy of 'Super'.

With less than ten minutes remaining before the necessity of extra time, witness the magic: a long David Robertson throw-in to a crowded Hibs' penalty area followed by an opportunist overhead kick by McCoist when virtually surrounded by four men in green. Despite a despairing Leighton dive to try to change the course of events, history was made.

The first leg of what could become a unique back-to-back 'Treble' was secure. Never having been achieved before in Scottish football, for Rangers it was now a possibility. League form would certainly have to improve and, of course, anything could happen in the Scottish Cup.

However, these thoughts were for the months ahead, since this day rightly belonged to the player worshipped by the Ibrox legions and affectionately known to many as 'the greatest-ever living Ranger', Alistair McCoist. ⚽

Rangers' first goal, courtesy of 'Blue, White, Dynamite', Ian Durrant.

RANGERS: Maxwell, Stevens, Robertson, Gough, McPherson, McCall, Steven, Ferguson, Durrant, Hateley, Huistra (McCoist).

PHOTO

FUN

QUIZ

1. Opposite: No flab here, just a jersey that seems too small! Who is it?

2. Below: Name the player with the balance of a ballet dancer seen scoring against Celtic.

3. If you want to get ahead, get a hat! Name the substitute warming up.

Answers on Page 64.

HEIR APPARENT

Duncan Ferguson

IT was a long time coming but when at last, the moment arrived, that massive home support rose as one to acknowledge a new beginning.

No prizes for guessing that it was Duncan Ferguson's first (first-team) goal for Rangers since his arrival in a blaze of publicity from Dundee United the previous close season. The record books would show that 'Dunc's' contribution was part of a comprehensive 4–0 victory over Raith Rovers at Ibrox in April '94.

The player himself was convinced his special moment had come some seven months earlier (against Partick Thistle at Ibrox) but celebrations then were short-lived as his first 'strike' was ruled off-side.

It had not been the easiest of times – injury seemed to shadow him for much of the season, limiting his number of appearances. There is little doubt, however, that a fully fit Duncan Ferguson will prove to be a major asset to both his club and country in their respective quests for European glory.

When his time comes, as surely it will, he'll be ready. ⚽

Premier League, 1st January 1994

CELTIC 2   RANGERS 4
Hateley (1 minute)
Mikhailitchenko (4 mins, 28 mins)
Kuznetsov (76 mins)

IN less than five minutes of this traditional New Year's Day 'Old Firm' encounter, Celtic had been blown away. By then Rangers were two goals ahead and simply cruising to victory.

Much of the pre-match talk had concerned the Celtic revival under new manager and former player, Lou Macari. Since taking charge, his team had not lost a single goal at Parkhead in seven matches. The home side were the favourites of many to take the day – after all, only two months earlier, Macari had watched his team come from a goal behind to win 2–1 at Ibrox . . . and this his first game in charge! Although Celtic had not won this January fixture since 1988, the omens seemed good for them.

Rangers, on the other hand, had not been playing consistently well. They were still without first-choice 'keeper Andy Goram and 'Super' Ally up front, both slowly recovering from long-term injuries. Club captain Richard Gough had missed the previous two games through injury but, fit again, would lead the team out at Parkhead.

Nobody could have predicted such a sensational

beginning when, in only 58 seconds, a superb pass from Stuart McCall left the rampaging Mark Hateley with only Pat Bonner to beat. As the Celtic 'keeper attempted to narrow the angle, Rangers' striker supreme calmly curled a glorious left-foot shot into the net. There would be none sweeter than this, his twenty-first goal of the season.

Mark then proceeded to run the length of the park and acknowledge the acclaim of the Rangers legions at the other end of the ground . . .
that goal was for them.

Strike No. 2 in four minutes followed a similar pattern in build-up. On this occasion, Gordon Durie split the Celtic defence with a pass to the advancing Neil Murray on the run. Although Bonner did well to stop the midfielder's goal attempt with his right leg, he could do nothing when the well-positioned Mikhailitchenko joyously stroked the ball home for his first goal of the campaign. That, as they say, was that.

Before the half-hour was out, Rangers struck a third time. It began when Mark Hateley rose majestically above his marker to head a Gary Stevens ball back across the penalty area. Although Gordon Durie miskicked in front of goal, 'Miko' was once again on hand to steer the ball home. It had become a rout.

Needless to say, the half-time whistle was

greeted with differing emotions by the opposing fans.

Celtic saw a glimmer of hope when John Collins pulled a goal back right at the outset of the second period – but this was duly cancelled out by a quite magnificent right-foot dipping volley from substitute Oleg Kuznetsov with some fifteen minutes remaining.

Nicholas's second Celtic goal near the end was really of no consequence as the points by this time had already been allocated.

After Rangers' 1–0 victory in the corresponding fixture at Ibrox the previous January, many neutrals had observed that Celtic had enjoyed the bulk of play. This was not to be the case this time, as the Ibrox club had clearly dominated the game from start to finish. Quite simply, Rangers came, saw and conquered with one of those special, all-round team performances.

Maybe the weathermen should have issued a storm alert before kick-off as the east end of Glasgow had surely witnessed a 'Tempest in Blue'.

JUST LIKE A HURRICANE. ⚽

> **RANGERS:** **Maxwell, Stevens, Murray (Kuznetsov), Gough, Pressley, Brown, Steven, McCall, Durie (Huistra), Hateley, Mikhailitchenko.**

Opposite: Mark Hateley celebrates his stunning first-minute strike at Parkhead, New Year's Day 1994.

MAGICAL "MIKO"

JUST picture the scene. Two obviously delighted Rangers' supporters, with grins the length of Copland Road, are reluctantly leaving Ibrox after the emphatic 4—1 victory over Celtic on 3rd January, 1989. One turns to the other and says:

"The next time we take four goals off Celtic in a Ne'erday match, three of them will be scored by Ukrainians!"

Happy in the knowledge that Glasgow's Southern General Hospital is nearby, his friend suggests a short detour for a quick check-up — from the neck up.

Yet it all came to pass in the 4—2 victory at Parkhead, January 1994, with Mikhailitchenko scoring goals 2 and 3 in that extraordinary first half and fellow-countryman Kuznetsov claiming No.4 late on in the second period.

Certainly 'Miko' couldn't have chosen a better time to score his first goals of the season. In fact, the double along with his equalising strike in the following encounter at Ibrox in April, ensured that the elegant playmaker was Rangers' top scorer against Celtic for season 1993/94.

Few punters would have predicted that at the beginning of the campaign. ⚽

'Miko' scoring against Raith Rovers and Celtic (Below), both matches in April 1994.

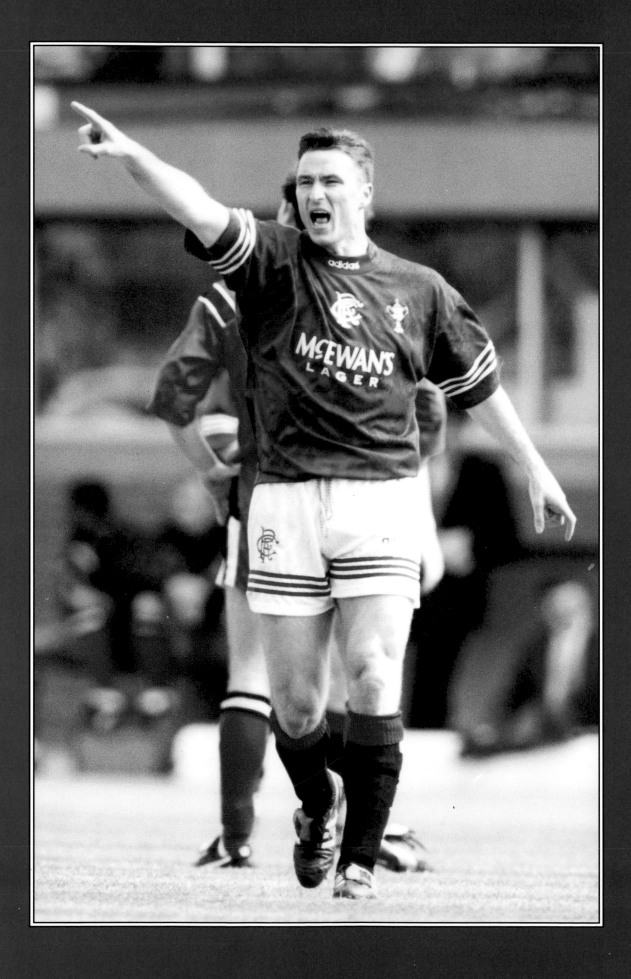

A DEEP SHADE OF BLUE

MANY fans still recall with relish the pre-season challenge game at the start of Season 1989/90 when Paul 'Gazza' Gascoigne (then with Tottenham Hotspur) was literally played off the park by Ian Ferguson. One of those masterly midfield performances that are an absolute joy to watch was witnessed that warm August day.

'Fergie's' light certainly shone again in Season 1993/94 with a series of powerful, hard-running midfield displays and, we should not forget, some extremely important goals for his beloved Rangers.

Certainly one of his nine strikes was one of the goals of the season – a cracking *left-foot* shot from just outside the box in the first minute of extra time to send Aberdeen reeling out of the League Cup.

Likewise it was Ian Ferguson's goal that had finally ended Aberdeen's Championship aspirations the previous season when a similar 25-yard drive found the net in Rangers' 2–0 March victory at Ibrox. Though on that occasion, it had been a more typical right-foot stunner!

It is common knowledge that 'Fergie' is a Rangers man through and through. Somehow it would come as no great surprise to be told that his heart pounds blue blood through those veins.

A DEEP SHADE OF TRUE BLUE, naturally. ⚽

A Touch of Class

TRULY gifted footballers are a rare breed in the Scottish game at present. Although a few names may spring to mind, scarcely anybody would question Trevor Steven's rightful inclusion within this elite band.

His abundance of sheer style shone through in a genuinely class performance as part of the Rangers team which lifted the season's first silverware in the League Cup Final.

Certainly most of the glory that day belonged to 'Super' but Steven's contribution nevertheless was highly significant controlling the midfield. Not only was his distribution superb but the player came close to scoring on no less than three occasions only to be foiled by the on-form Jim Leighton of Hibernian.

A succession of injuries blighted his season, the final straw being a troublesome groin ensuring that he missed the Scottish Cup Final.

Trevor Steven has played in four F.A. Cup Finals at Wembley (victory once for Everton against Watford but defeat on three occasions: against Liverpool, twice, and Manchester United) but has yet to appear in the corresponding fixture in Scotland.

Hopefully this will be rectified before too long as surely Scottish Cup Final day cries out for players of his undoubted calibre to grace the Hampden turf. ⚽

Trevor Steven scored 6 goals in season 1993/94.
Shown above is his aerial strike in the 5–1 victory
over Partick Thistle at Ibrox, February 1994.

GOAL!

GOAL!

*Above: Mark's winner for ten-man Rangers in
the League Cup semi-final at Ibrox.*

*Below: 'That' first-minute goal at
Parkhead, New Year's Day 1994.*

*Above: Ally celebrates his
goal at Ibrox,
November 1993.*

*Below: 'Dunc's' goal for the reserves
before a 20,000
crowd at Ibrox.*

Walter Smith, Archie Knox and Davie Dodds take a bow.

Scotland's Player of the Year 1994

Another close thing in the final home match of the season.
Below: That 6-in-a Row Championship feeling!

'6-IN-A-ROW'

Season 1988/89

1. *Name the player who made his 'Old Firm' debut in August and scored in the same match.*

2. *What was the result of that first game v. Celtic?*

3. *Which team knocked Rangers out of the U.E.F.A. Cup?*

4. *Give the score (and scorers) in the traditional 'Ne'erday' game.*

Season 1989/90

1. *His signing caused quite a stir. Who was he?*

2. *Name the midfield player who joined from Everton.*

3. *At which ground did Rangers win the Championship?*

4. *Who was the Club's top scorer?*

Season 1990/91

1. *Who scored Rangers' second goal in that memorable last game of the season against Aberdeen?*

2. *Name the new signing who only lasted 96 minutes before missing the rest of the season through injury.*

3. *Two influential personalities left the Club this season. Who were they?*

4. *The team that put Rangers out of the European Cup went on to win the Trophy. True or False?*

FUN QUIZ

Season 1991/92

1. Who finished runners-up to Rangers in the League?

2. Rangers created a Premier League goalscoring record this season. How many goals were scored in the campaign?

3. Which players joined Rangers from the following clubs: a) Hibernian? b) Norwich? c) Notts County?

4. Who scored his 200th League goal this year?

Season 1992/93

1. Who scored for Rangers against Marseille in both European Cup matches?

2. At what ground did Rangers secure the Championship?

3. Ally's front-line partnership with Mark Hateley netted how many goals?

4. The 'Treble' was won for the first time since ... when?

Season 1993/94

1. There really can be only one question –

   HOW MANY MORE?

Answers on page 64

The Glory Guy

AN OLD proverb reminds us that, *'You never miss the water until the well runs dry'*. Rangers' main source (of goals) never actually dried up in the early stages of season 1993/94 – he just wasn't available. The player in question, Ally McCoist, had totalled an amazing 49 strikes the previous year – some 'well'!

One of several regulars missing through injury at that time, 'Super' would eventually return to first-team football in the humble surroundings of Starks Park, Kirkcaldy in October. Injury, however, would return to haunt him again the following month.

Regardless of this – or maybe even *because* of it – Ally was never far from glory when he did appear on the park. Certainly, a crowd of over 47,000 would bear witness to this as they viewed the most dramatic of winning goals against Hibernian at Parkhead which returned the League Cup to the Ibrox Trophy Room. 'His Greatness' had struck again!

Also particularly worth remembering was his stunning late, late strike against Partick Thistle at Firhill on a miserable cold, wet night in what was a most important victory in the run-in to the '6-IN-A-ROW' 1993/94 Premier Championship.

Though it was far from a vintage McCoist season, then, for obvious reasons, no doubt the man himself would remind us of big Arnie's 'Terminator' promise: **"I'll be back!"** ⚽

The Glory Guy

Above: Ally scoring that late, late goal against Thistle, March 1994.
Below: 'The Glory Guy' salutes Ian Ferguson's equaliser against Raith Rovers, February 1994.

TERRY BUTCHER

Terry celebrates with Kevin Drinkell his powerful headed goal v. Celtic, Parkhead, August 1989 depicted opposite (above).

The opening goal at Celtic Park which triggered the Butcher celebrations opposite.

Championship celebrations at Tannadice, April 1990.

Signed from Ipswich Town in August 1986, Terry Butcher that season captained Rangers to their first League Championship since 1978 and went on to become one of the club's truly great leaders.

BATTLE CRY

IN many ways it was like a call to arms. Morale had inevitably been affected by that demoralising 3–0 home defeat at the hands of Dundee United in December. There had been precious little festive cheer that day as those pre-Christmas bells clearly sounded out a warning to the Ibrox club.

The gauntlet had been thrown down, the challenge made but, as had been proved so often over the last few years, Rangers would be more than ready to face all pretenders to their throne.

The 'Light Blues' then embarked on a 22 match unbeaten run which included comprehensive and satisfying victories over Celtic, Motherwell and Hibernian. Before the sequence ended at the end of April, the blue and red ribbons on another Championship trophy were already within sight.

To many, this had been the most satisfying title of all six. The seemingly never-ending list of injuries had been quite horrendous. In fact, before the season was finished, the following players would require hospitalisation and operations – Andy Goram, Ally McCoist, Gary Stevens, Trevor Steven, John Brown, Stuart McCall, Dave McPherson, Duncan Ferguson, David Robertson, Ian Durrant and Richard Gough.

The record books will show that Walter Smith's players had become the first Rangers team ever to win six consecutive League Championships.

AND THAT'S A FACT! ⚽

LEGEND

Scottish Cup Semi-Final, 13th April 1994

KILMARNOCK   1   RANGERS   2

Hateley (47, 52 mins)

THIS semi-final replay can be summed up in three words: Mark and Hateley.

It came as no surprise that it was the towering, intimidating 'Hit Man' who finally rescued Rangers to keep the dream alive. Hateley struck twice in the space of five frantic minutes early in the second half after Kilmarnock had led by a single goal at the break.

The 'Dark Destroyer's' first goal (a lethal downward header from an Ian Durrant cross) was his 29th of the season, thus equalling his career best from the previous year. Five minutes later, that personal record would be broken.

His second strike was courtesy of fine, powerful running down the left flank by Gordon Durie, as he literally brushed Kilmarnock defenders aside before crossing for 'Top Mark' to steer home with his left foot. Hampden was beckoning again for a Cup Final date with Dundee United on the last day of the season, the Taysiders, surprisingly, having lost all six of their previous Scottish Cup Finals at the National Stadium.

A fool might question the accolades heaped upon Mark Hateley but to those privileged to watch him throughout season 1993/94 and before, it was quite apparent that this celebrated Ranger was fast becoming a legend in his own time. ⚽

RANGERS: Maxwell, McCall, Robertson, Gough, McPherson, Pressley, Durie, I. Ferguson, McCoist, Hateley, Durrant (Huistra).

RAY   WILKINS

Ray Wilkins joined Rangers from Paris St Germain in 1987 after having previously played for both Manchester United and A.C. Milan.

A superbly gifted midfield player, Wilkins became such a favourite that when he left Rangers in December 1989 (to return south for family reasons) he was given a standing ovation at Ibrox at the end of his final game for the club.

Ray is visibly moved by the reception at Ibrox following his last game for Rangers.

Opposite (Above): Ray in action against UEFA Cup opponents Katowice of Poland at Ibrox, September 1988.

Opposite (Below): Wilkins clashes with Roddy Grant of St Johnstone.

47

BLUE HEAVEN

*Extracts from the illustrated book
of the Ibrox Trophy Room
by Rangers' legend*
Willie Thornton

SPODE CHINA BOWL

1961

This exquisite gift was presented by Wolverhampton Wanderers to mark the occasion of the Cup Winners' Cup semi-final joust of 1961. Wolves were one of the pre-tournament favourites, having won the English First Division twice in the previous three seasons.

Rangers won the first leg at Ibrox 2–0 before an 80,000 crowd. These were the days before substitutes and iron man Harold Davis had to limp out the match on the right wing after a ninth minute injury. Despite this setback, goals from Scott and Brand won the day.

Heavy snow made the ground slippery and treacherous for the Molyneux return, which ended in a 1–1 draw, leaving Rangers victorious. A memorable moment came in the dying minutes of the first half, when Billy Ritchie made an almost unbelievable save from a rasping Ron Flowers drive, allowing Rangers to go in 3–0 ahead on aggregate.

This fine result made Rangers the first British team to reach a European final. It also helped restore some of the pride and credibility of Scottish football, coming as it did just four days after the 9–3 Wembley humiliation of our international squad. No doubt the backing of an astonishing travelling support of 10,000 was a significant factor in the heroic Rangers performance.

March 29th: First Leg   Rangers 2   Wolves 0
Scott (33)
Brand (84)

RANGERS: Ritchie; Shearer, Caldow; Davis, Paterson, Baxter; Scott, Wilson, Baillie, Brand, Hume.

April 19th: Second Leg   Wolves 1   Rangers 1
Scott (43)

RANGERS: Ritchie; Shearer, Caldow; Davis, Paterson, Baxter; Wilson, McMillan, Scott, Brand, Hume.

Rangers won 3–1 on aggregate.

Height 7″ (17.75cms)

THE LOVING CUP
1937

If the Trophy Room is the crowning glory of Ibrox, then The Loving Cup is the Jewel in the Crown. One of only thirty cast from a unique mould (subsequently destroyed) to commemorate the coronation in May 1937 of Their Majesties King George VI and Queen Elizabeth (later Queen Mother), the story of how it came into Rangers' possession is part of the club's folklore.

Identical Loving Cups were presented to the 22 English First Division clubs of the time, with the remainder going to the British Museum and various organisations.

Then, as now, Rangers were recognised as one of the world's great clubs and so it was that they were asked to participate in a special match to raise funds for the dependants of the miners who lost their lives in the Holditch Colliery Disaster, in the Stoke area. Manager Struth accepted the invitation with alacrity.

Stoke City President, Sir Francis Joseph, gifted Rangers his own club's Loving Cup in appreciation after the match, which was goalless. He requested that the vessel should be used in perpetuity to drink to the health of the reigning monarch on the occasion of our first home match of every year. So it is that to this day, the New Year toast is celebrated in the Blue Room by the assembled directors and guests of Rangers and their first visiting opponents.

As far as can be ascertained, the Rangers Loving Cup is one of the very few remaining and probably the only one still in regular use.

October 19th, 1937:   **Stoke City 0   Rangers 0**

RANGERS: Dawson; Gray, McDonald; McKillop, Simpson, Little; Main, Fiddes, Smith, Venters, Kinnear.

Height 6½″ (16.5cms)

**The Loving Cup
1937**

THERE'S

ONE

ONLY

MARK
HATELEY

STUART McCALL

SCOTLAND

AND

One Day in May

Scottish Cup Final, 21st May 1994

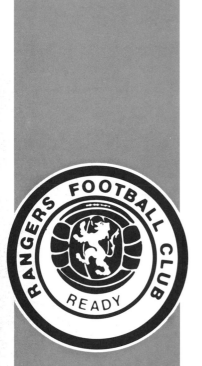

A LITTLE bit of history would be in the making this day regardless of the colour of the victory ribbons adorning the old trophy. Rangers could become the first team ever to secure consecutive 'trebles', whereas their opponents might finally end their Scottish Cup 'hoodoo' of never having lifted the trophy, in this, their seventh Final appearance since 1974.

From a neutral point of view, it was a fascinating contest. Although the Taysiders had arguably the better of the first half, it was Rangers who came nearest to scoring, when Dave McPherson's net-bound header was cleared off the line by McInally with Van De Kamp well beaten.

The scenario changed dramatically – maybe even farcically – when Brewster accepted a gift and scored two minutes into the second half following a defensive muddle.

Rangers now surged forward incessantly but that elusive equaliser never materialised despite good efforts from both Hateley and 'Miko'.

At the end of the day, it just wasn't meant to be but it was hard to take, coming so tantalisingly close to triple glory again. ⚽

ANGERS: Maxwell, Stevens (Mikhailitchenko 24 mins), Robertson, Gough, McPherson, McCall, Murray, I. Ferguson, McCoist (D. Ferguson 73 mins), Hateley, Durie.

Duncan Ferguson

Neil Murray

Gordon Durie

'BOMBER 2

FEW would dispute that John Brown made himself the true 'heart' of the Ibrox back four. Like the missing piece of a jigsaw, Rangers' defences of recent years have seemed somehow incomplete without 'Bomber' wearing his customary No.6 jersey.

Sadly, as with several other players from the first-team squad, injury played a major role in the early part of John's '93/'94 year. Additionally, a troublesome groin ensured that he also missed the last few games of the season, including the Scottish Cup Final against Dundee United in May.

All the same, 'Bomber' did provide one awesome moment of genuine satisfaction — his only goal of the season, certainly, but surely one of the year's most memorable.

Early in the second half of what was proving to be a most difficult quarter-final Scottish Cup tie at Ibrox, John unleashed a devastatingly ferocious left-foot strike from some 30 yards to open the scoring and send Rangers on their way to Hampden. The sponsor's 'Man of the Match' award that day was his.

Somehow it's more than enough just to say: **John Brown, Rangers.** ⚽

Opposite: (Above) 'Bomber' in action against Partick Thistle at Firhill.
(Below) John Brown dispossesses his namesake Tom, of Kilmarnock, at Rugby Park.

JOHN

BROWN

FUN QUIZ

Season 1993/94

1. *'Hit Man' Hateley scored 30 goals in the season. How many of these were 'Doubles'?*

2. *What was unusual about the League Cup semi-final played at Ibrox?*

3. *Who was Rangers' top scorer v. Celtic?*

4. *What is the English link between Gordon Durie and Richard Gough?*

5. *In the current Rangers squad, who has won the most League Cup winner's medals?*

6. *Rangers scored 4 goals on 4 occasions during the season. Can you list the games?*

7. *The attendance v. Partick Thistle was higher than the number of spectators v. Levski Sofia in the European Cup match at Ibrox the following week. True or False?*

8. *His only goal of the season was in the opening game v. Hearts at Ibrox. Name the player.*

9. *Only one player appeared in the starting line-up for Rangers' first 29 games of the season. Who was he?*

10. *What was unusual about Mark Hateley's appearance as substitute against Raith Rovers on 16th April, 1994?*

Answers on Page 64

ANSWERS

FUN QUIZ

1. 8 (Levski Sofia 15.9.93; Hearts 3.11.93 and 27.12.93; Raith Rovers 13.11.93; Aberdeen 1.12.93; St Johnstone 18.12.93; Kilmarnock 8.1.94 and 13.4.94.)

2. Celtic fans were allocated both Broomloan and Govan Stands.

3. Alexei Mikhailitchenko with 3 goals.

4. Both players joined Rangers from Tottenham Hotspur.

5. Ally McCoist with 8.

6. St Johnstone 18.12.93 and 19.3.94; Dumbarton 29.1.94; Celtic 1.1.94.

7. True. 40,998 compared to 37,013.

8. David Hagen.

9. Ian Ferguson.

10. Replacing the injured David Robertson, 'Hit Man' slotted into the centre of defence with John Brown moving to left back.

'6-IN-A-ROW' FUN QUIZ

Season 1988/89

1. Kevin Drinkell.

2. 5–1 McCoist (2), Wilkins, Drinkell and Walters.

3. Cologne.

4. 4–1 Walters (2), Butcher and Ian Ferguson.

Season 1989/90

1. Maurice Johnston.

2. Trevor Steven.

3. Tannadice.

4. Maurice Johnston with 21 goals.

Season 1990/91

1. Mark Hateley.

2. Oleg Kuznetsov.

3. Terry Butcher and Graeme Souness.

4. True. Red Star Belgrade defeated Marseille in the Final that year.

Season 1991/92

1. Hearts with 63 points.

2. 101 goals.

3. a) Andy Goram b) Dale Gordon c) Paul Rideout.

4. Ally McCoist.

Season 1992/93

1. Gary McSwegan; Mark Hateley (Ibrox); Ian Durrant (France).

2. Broomfield.

3. An amazing 78 goals.

4. 1978.

PHOTO FUN QUIZ

1. Duncan Ferguson when he thought he'd just scored his first goal for Rangers v. Partick Thistle.

2. Alexei Mikhailitchenko scoring goal No.3 against Celtic, January 1994.

3. Ally McCoist.

ACKNOWLEDGEMENTS

Designed by Douglas Russell and John Traynor, with special assistance from Lisa Russell.

Typesetting and Origination by Inglis Allen, Kirkcaldy.

Bound in Scotland by Hunter & Foulis, Edinburgh.

All photographs supplied by *The Sun* except pages 48 & 51, reproduced from 'Blue Heaven', published 1991 by Holmes McDougall Ltd.

Every effort has been made by the publishers to ensure the accuracy of all details and information in this publication.

Printed and Published in Scotland by

INGLIS ALLEN

40 Townsend Place, Kirkcaldy, Fife, Scotland KY1 1HF.

ISBN 0-9519694-5-5 © Inglis Allen 1994. All rights reserved.